Safari
Journal

Boyd Norton, Edward Borg,
Ed Sokolosky, and Stephanie Sokolosky

Fulcrum Publishing
Golden, Colorado

Library of Congress Cataloging-in-Publication Data

Safari journal / Boyd Norton ...[et al.].
    p. cm.
    ISBN-13: 978-1-55591-586-5 (pbk.)
    ISBN-10: 1-55591-586-8
    1. Safaris. 2. Safaris--Africa. I. Norton, Boyd.
    G516.S24 2007
    916.04'33—dc22

                                        2006022959

Printed in China by C&C Offset Printing Co., Ltd.
0 9 8 7 6 5 4 3 2 1
Editorial: Faith Marcovecchio
Design: Patty Maher

Fulcrum Publishing
4690 Table Mountain Drive, Suite 100
Golden, Colorado 80403
800-992-2908 • 303-277-1623
www.fulcrumbooks.com

Contents

Marabou storks resting in the top of an acacia tree. There are numerous varieties of acacias, all with fine, feathery leaves and most with long, sharp thorns as defense against browsers. Despite the thorns, giraffes feed on acacia leaves, using their leathery tongues to strip them from between thorns.

Introduction

The word *safari* comes from a very old African language, Swahili. It simply means "journey" or "trip." However, in modern times, the term has new connotations, recalling certain traditions of elegance and excitement in traveling through the remote African bush. It brings to mind scenes of Robert Redford and Meryl Streep in *Out of Africa*. And it makes each of us envision great herds of animals ranging across limitless savanna where predators lie in wait. The safari tradition is carried out today in many parts of Africa.

In few other places can you find such country to stimulate the mind and imagination. To remind yourself later of the adventures and wonders of your safari, you'll want to keep a personal journal of your impressions. That's part of the purpose of this safari journal.

Undoubtedly, you will want to capture the beauty and excitement of it all with your camera, whether it's digital, film, or video. Another aim of the *Safari Journal* is to help you with that visual record by providing useful tips and advice on photography—by sharing with you our combined experiences of several decades' worth of photographing the wonders of this continent.

Still a third purpose is to provide information on preparing for your journey: the best time to go to certain countries and areas, what to bring, how to pack, health and medical considerations, and more. Traveling in most parts of Africa is different from ordinary vacations—but then, that's part of the reason for going.

Finally, to make your trip most meaningful, we've provided checklists of some of the more common birds and animal life you'll encounter. The photos and captions here will serve not only to help identify some of the varied species, they will give insight into behavior and characteristics that make African wildlife unique.

BOYD NORTON

A black rhino. Black rhinos are not necessarily black. They take on the color of the dust or mud in which they last rolled. Black rhinos are browsers with a narrow and prehensile upper lip, useful in feeding on the woody stems and twigs of plants.

Preparing for Your Safari

Trip Prep. Checklist:

☐ **Make flight arrangements early.** In recent years, flights have been filling quickly for peak-season travel. Airline reservations should be made as early as possible to ensure seat availability and the best possible price. Keep in mind that the heaviest travel seasons are different for different parts of Africa. In East Africa, peak travel occurs in January and February and June through August. In southern Africa, popular travel takes place in November through March.

☐ **Get a passport.** If you do not already have a passport, you need to apply for one well before departure. If you do have one, make sure it will remain valid for at least six months after the date of your return from Africa. (This is a requirement for entry into many, if not most, countries these days.)

☐ **Check on visa requirements.** As of this writing, most countries in East Africa require visas, though in some cases you can obtain one upon arrival. Be sure to check first. South Africa does not require a visa. The best source for visa information is on the U.S. State Department Web site: http://travel.state.gov/travel/travel_1744.html. **Note:** Some countries may require certification of yellow fever vaccination if you are coming from countries in South America or sub-Saharan Africa. If you apply for a visa beforehand, be sure to allow plenty of time for processing before your trip begins.

☐ **Take the necessary health precautions.** There is no reason to fear traveling in Africa if you take proper health precautions. The best source for health information for travelers is the Centers for Disease Control and Prevention Web site: www.cdc.gov. Malaria is the greatest concern, but effective drugs and use of insect repellent can prevent it. Consult with your physician for advice on travel medications and precautionary items to take with you. If your health insurance does not cover international medical treatment, you need to secure additional medical coverage to play it safe.

❑ **Get a dental checkup.** A broken or lost filling can ruin a trip. Get everything checked out before you go. Consult with your dentist about purchasing a dental emergency kit. These kits usually contain temporary fillings, cements for crowns or caps, and some toothache medication.

❑ **Bring extra eyeglasses and contact lenses.** In addition to extra glasses, you may want to bring an eyeglass repair kit. If your soft contact lenses require treatment in an electric sterilizer, be sure to bring appropriate plug adapters and a 220-volt transformer. (See page 5 for more information on electrical appliances.) Dust is inevitable in your travels in Africa, and for contact lens wearers, it can be uncomfortable. Bring an ample supply of lens lubricant.

❑ **Bring an ample supply of any medications you take.** Always keep medications (and passport and important papers) in your carry-on bag for all flights, international and regional. Make sure you have enough medication to tide you over if there are flight or trip delays.

What to Bring
and How to Pack It

P̄ack lightly. There is no need for a fashion statement on safari, and you can get by with very casual and comfortable clothing. Many people envision all of Africa as being hot and steamy. While that's true in some places on the continent, you will find many areas in East and southern Africa to have very moderate climate—warm, perhaps hot days, but cool, if not chilly nights. In such places as Ngorongoro Crater in Tanzania, the elevation (7,500 feet above sea level) can make for very chilly evenings and mornings. The same is true in some of the upland regions of South Africa. Check with your safari outfitter for information on weather and climate conditions.

Layered clothing makes the most sense in places with varied temperatures: shorts and T-shirts during the day, and for those cool evenings and mornings, fleece jackets or sweaters and long pants. Most safari lodges and camps have laundry facilities (check with your safari or tour company). It is often suggested that wearing khaki or neutral-colored clothing is best because white or bright colors frighten the animals. This is, of course, nonsense. However, khaki does hide the dirt and dust better!

For footwear, comfort is again the key—wear tennis shoes, sandals, lightweight hiking shoes, or whatever you prefer. If you are trekking, you will definitely need good hiking boots. And for rain forest trekking, as in mountain-gorilla visits in Rwanda or Uganda, you will want waterproof boots and good rain gear.

In most places, the African sun is intense, especially in East Africa on or near the equator. Take along a broad-brimmed hat for protection and a good supply of sunscreen for exposed skin.

If you pack your items in zippered duffle bags, as opposed to hard-sided suitcases, it will save some weight. However, if you plan to bring back any delicate items, you may want to use at least one hard-sided suitcase for

Packing Checklist:

- ❏ Small but powerful flashlight; LCD flashlights pack the most power for weight and size.
- ❏ Binoculars for game-viewing
- ❏ Hat, scarf, and bandanna (the latter to cover nose against dust)
- ❏ Sunscreen and insect repellent
- ❏ Premoistened face towels
- ❏ Facial tissues
- ❏ Transformer and adapter plugs (see page 5 for information on electrical appliances)
- ❏ Spare glasses and contact lenses
- ❏ Glasses repair kit
- ❏ Camera(s), lenses, film, extra batteries, battery charger (see photography section, pages 25–33)
- ❏ Two pairs of sunglasses
- ❏ Camera vest or jacket (all the pockets are very handy, even if you aren't a photographer)
- ❏ Bathing suit (many lodges and camps have swimming pools)
- ❏ Guidebooks (birds, mammals, and so on). Check with your safari outfitter; many have guidebooks for sale, thus saving you from carrying them to Africa.
- ❏ Two pairs of footwear: tennis shoes for daytime, sandals for lounging in the evenings
- ❏ Basic first-aid kit with Band-aids, antiseptic, ointments, aspirin or equivalent, stomach medications, tweezers, and so on
- ❏ Prescription medications
- ❏ Clothing—**For men:** Shorts, T-shirts or polo shirts, pair of long pants, short-sleeved shirts, long-sleeved shirts, casual semi-dress pants and shirt for evening dinners at lodges. **For women:** Shorts or long pants, comfortable shirts, pullovers, or T-shirts (both long- and short-sleeved), casual semi-dress blouse and skirt for evening dinners at lodges. **For both sexes:** Socks and underwear for the duration of the trip, keeping in mind laundry facility availability (check with your safari/travel company)

- ❏ Sweater or sweatshirt
- ❏ Lightweight jacket
- ❏ Rain jacket, with rain pants for gorilla trekking
- ❏ Plastic bags in assorted sizes: medium-sized to put cameras in to protect them against dust and rain, large trash bags to slip over camera bags to keep out dust from the road
- ❏ Several sheets of bubble wrap to carefully wrap delicate items you may purchase on safari (carvings, masks, and so on)
- ❏ Personal toiletry kit
- ❏ Your copy of *Safari Journal* to record the impressions of your journey!

better protection. Commercial airlines have liberal policies on number of checked bags and weight, but bear in mind that your safari may entail some local travel on small aircraft with very stringent weight limitations. Check with your safari outfitter or tour company and commercial airlines.

Regarding electrical appliances: all over the African continent, the electricity is 220 to 240 volts. For North American travelers, this requires either a transformer to convert the higher voltage to 110 volts or appliances that are dual voltage (automatically switchable between the two voltages). Most digital camera and video battery chargers are dual voltage, but check the label to be sure. You will also need adapter plugs to fit the sockets.

Electrical adapters vary from country to country. Check this Web site for more specific information for the countries you'll visit:
http://users.pandora.be/worldstandards/electricity.htm.

East African
electrical plug

In parts of southern Africa, these type of plugs are used.

EDWARD BORG

Among the big cats, leopards are always prized sightings on safari. Shy and elusive, they rest during the day in trees, waiting for the cover of night to hunt gazelles or impala. They often drag their kill up into a tree to prevent lions or hyenas from stealing their meal.

On Safari

Many years afterward they would come up to the house and
talk about the safari, just to freshen their memory of it, and to
go through one or another of our adventures ...
                                        —*Karen Blixen*, Out of Africa

To be on safari in Africa is like stepping back in time and seeing the world when it was young.

The traditional safari experience originated in East Africa, where the grasslands and savannas are indeed expansive and seemingly limitless. When you travel to southern Africa, there is less savanna and more forest and brushland, but the safari tradition is kept very much the same here. Incidentally, in southern Africa, savanna is referred to as *veld* or *veldt*, a word derived from Dutch meaning "field." In either of these two regions of Africa, the land and wildlife are varied. In addition to the savannas or velds, there are thick forests, crackling dry deserts, great rivers and lakes, high mountains, and a grand feeling of spaciousness. With the variation in ecosystems, there are variations in the animal and birdlife as well.

Your visit to the game parks and reserves is a chance to rediscover the wonders and beauty of the natural world. There's also a chance outside the parks to experience some of Africa's rich and varied cultural heritage. Take this opportunity to expand your senses and absorb the sights, sounds, and aromas that make up this fascinating part of the world.

Far removed from modern culture, life goes on in the plains and forests of Africa as it has for millennia. On the surface of it all, things seem pretty simple here. Three primary elements dictate the survival of every-thing: sunlight, water, and plants. Sun and rain nurture grasses and brush. The numerous herbivores feed on this plant life. The predators, in turn, feed on the herbivores.

From this seemingly simple arrangement springs an incredibly complex web of life. As you travel on safari, take note of the many things going on around you, such as the role played by scavengers such as jackals and vultures after predators have made their kill and eaten. Other things are not so apparent. For example, the lowly dung beetle gathers animal dung, rolling it into balls that it pushes along until the right spot is found, then the beetle buries the ball deep in the soil. In this process, the beetle feeds itself and its larvae, plus fertilizes and aerates the roots of life-giving grasses. Multiply this simple act millions of times, and you can see that as a species, the dung beetle plays an important role in the ecosystem here. There are many other equally important and diverse species.

Throughout much of the continent roam vast herds of grazers, members of the antelope and gazelle families, and these herbivores play distinctive roles in the plant ecosystems. Through a process known as grazing succession, different herbivores utilize different grasses and convert grasslands for other grazers to use. When the grasses are tall, elephants and buffalo graze heavily, eating and trampling the tall, coarse stems and tops. This makes it possible for fresh new shoots to emerge. Soon zebras and hippos may feed on the remaining coarse grasses, exposing still more fresh shoots. Finally, the wildebeest and gazelles move in to feed on these preferred green shoots.

Though their numbers were greatly reduced by poaching during the 1980s, elephants have made a comeback over parts of the continent, thanks to the international ban on ivory sales. As you can observe on your safari, elephants prefer a habitat of mixed woodland and grassland, giving them opportunity to eat a variety of vegetation. They are both browsers and grazers; they will eat rough sticks, stems and leaves of plants, as well as grasses and sedges and, when available, fruit. In woodlands, elephants eat the bark, twigs, and leaves of trees. Because of their great size and strength, they are often able to knock down trees to get at the green canopy normally out of their reach. As a result, a large number of elephants in a given area can kill most of the trees. This, in turn, opens up dense woodlands, converting the habitat to grasslands. The elephants, when not restricted by human encroachment, move on to other woodlands, and the population of grazing animals in their previous habitat then increases.

Elephants band together in family groups led by a wise old matriarch, who passes along to the next generation the secrets of survival, as elephants have done for eons. From her, the youngsters learn where to find water in times of drought and where the best vegetation can be found at different times of year. Elephant families are made up of mothers and daughters of various ages together with males that have not yet reached puberty. Daughters will often remain with the family unit all of their lives, but males leave when they reach puberty, at about twelve to fourteen years of age.

The most common predators you'll find on safari are lions. These are the social members of the cat family. Somewhat like elephants, lions also live in distinct family units, called prides. The pride is made up of a number of related females and their cubs ranging over a large territory that may be anywhere from 50 to 150 square miles in area, depending on the terrain. The habitat can range from grasslands to savanna or veld (mixed woodlands and grasslands) to woodlands. At about three years of age, males are driven out of the pride, becoming nomads. When fully matured, the individual male may roam over very large areas that may include two or three prides, and he may mate with one or more of the females of these prides. If a strange male appears in the territory, a fight often ensues—sometimes with fatal consequences. Females of the pride may also drive off a foreign lioness if she enters their territory.

The female lions of a pride do the stalking and hunting, mostly at night. They often hunt cooperatively. During your safari, you may be fortunate enough to observe several lionesses setting a trap for an unwary grazer. Patiently, they will encircle their prey, sneaking through grass, crouched low to the ground, and freezing into immobility for minutes at a time. Even with such cunning tactics, the lion success rate for making a kill is less than 30 percent on average. If a kill is made, often the dominant male, if he is nearby, will chase away the females. Only after he has eaten his fill will he allow the females and cubs to eat. Lions are also scavengers, and sometimes they will chase hyenas or cheetahs away from their kills. But the most common behavior you will observe in lions is sleeping. During the heat of the day, the pride will sleep under a tree, lifting their heads only occasionally to check out the happenings on the vast, sun-drenched plain. The lion's daily life is often described as twenty-three hours of sleep followed by one hour of sheer terror for its prey.

As opposed to lion behavior, the cheetah is most active during the daytime. This is when they do their hunting, relying on tremendous speed—up to 70 miles per hour—to bring down a gazelle or young wilde-beest or baby zebra. However, these sleek and elegant cats cannot sustain such speeds for more than seconds at a time and, if they do not succeed in bringing down their prey quickly, they must give up the chase.

Cheetahs are generally loners, except for females with cubs. Occasionally two or three males (usually siblings) will travel and hunt together, though they will eventually part ways and each will go off on its own. Females can produce litters of up to six cubs, though three to four is most common. Cub mortality in cheetahs is high, with youngsters falling prey to other predators such as hyenas or lions. In years of drought and sparse prey, starvation is common. A female with cubs must hunt several times a day to keep her cubs healthy and to ensure their survival. Cheetahs often lose their kills to hyenas or lions, so the cub survival rate depends very much on the mother making many kills. This makes it especially important that safari vehicles not interfere with cheetahs (or other preda-tors) on a hunt. Vehicles approaching too closely can frighten off the animal that is being stalked. Too many such occurrences may jeopardize the survival of both cubs and adults.

Cheetah cubs will stay with their mother until they are about fifteen months of age. After that time, they will leave and go off on their own, sometimes traveling and hunting together for a while.

If you are lucky on your safari, you may be able to see one of the most elusive of the big cats: the leopard. These powerful and graceful animals are mostly hunters of the night. They spend daytime hours in a tree, sprawled across a limb, asleep in the cool shade. At dusk, the leopard awakens, yawns, stretches, and then noiselessly slips down from its lofty height to begin its hunt. Silently, like a ghost, it blends into the nighttime landscape. At dawn, it will be back in its tree, feeding on a Thomson's or a Grant's gazelle or an impala that it has hauled up into the branches. The fact that its kill sometimes weighs as much or more than the cat itself and is carried thirty feet or more up into a tree is testimony to the incredible strength of these animals. This behavior prevents hyenas or lions from stealing the leopard's kill.

Leopard territory is most commonly the woodland bordering streams and rivers; only rarely is it found in the grasslands. Spotting leopards resting in trees can test your powers of observation and your eyesight. Often, from a distance the only clue is a tail hanging down from tangled tree branches. If you have ever wondered why leopards have spots, look carefully at how the mottled pattern of their spots blends in with the mottled pattern of leaves behind them.

For all predators, the hunt can be a risky venture. Cheetahs may attempt to kill a baby wildebeest or zebra, but a defending mother wildebeest or zebra (far too big and powerful for the cheetah to take on) can deliver a dangerous, crippling blow by horn or hoof. Lions often undertake the seemingly suicidal task of killing a Cape buffalo and are sometimes fatally injured in the process. So even though the top of the food chain is dominated by fang and claw, life is never easy on these African plains or forests. As you will observe in your safari travels, nothing here is wasted; everything is recycled.

> White rhinos are not white, but, rather, the color of whatever mud or dust they rolled in last.

High on the wish list of safari travelers is sighting a rhino. Once prevalent all over the continent, these animals are, sadly, among the most endangered species in Africa. Though they are now heavily guarded in parks and reserves, poaching still takes place. The rhino horn, contrary to popular myth, is not sought after as an aphrodisiac but rather as a cure for fevers in Asia. The biggest market for the rhino horn is for dagger handles in the Arab world, where the horns command very high prices.

The white rhino is most prevalent in southern Africa. White rhinos are not white, but rather the color of whatever mud or dust they rolled in last. Moreover, the name itself is derived from the Dutch word *weidt*, meaning "wide." They are grazers, feeding on grasses of the plains or veld, and as such, their wide mouths aid in feeding on these plants. In contrast, black rhinos (which are not necessarily black) have narrow, pointed mouths with prehensile upper lips. Black rhinos are browsers, feeding on the woody stems of plants and on bark and leaves.

In certain protected areas of southern Africa, white rhino populations have increased enough to allow translocation to other regions. In some Kenyan parks, white rhinos have been transplanted, though the species was never native to Kenya (the northern white rhino was once found in Uganda). Until the myths of curative powers of rhino horn are dispelled and usage in dagger handles ends, the sad fact is that both black and white rhinos will still need much protection against poachers.

There's so much more that you may experience on your safari. Watch for the smaller animals, including jackals, bat-eared foxes, warthogs, and dik-diks. There are numerous smaller cats, such as the lovely serval and the hard-to-find caracal. The African wild cat may look amazingly like your own house cat (which is a distant relative), but it's highly adapted to life among huge animals and the bigger predators for which it may be prey.

Perhaps the least favorite animal is the hyena, with its slinky demeanor and voracious scavenging (they are also efficient hunters, often working in packs). However you may feel about them, hyenas are among the most observant mammals on the grasslands. Scanning the skies, they spot distant circling vultures and know that there's a kill to be found. Often you will see one or more hyenas racing across the grasslands for no apparent reason, but more than likely they are heading toward that kill.

If you are really lucky in your travels, you may have a chance of seeing the wild dog, also called the Cape hunting dog. These are not feral

ED SOKOLOSKY

Rhinos, both black and white, have become Africa's most endangered species. Once numbering in the hundreds of thousands across the continent, their numbers have plummeted to fewer than 4,000 in the past few decades. These black rhinos are well protected in Tanzania's Ngorongoro Crater.

dogs, but true wild dogs. They have been called painted wolves for their variegated coloring and pack behavior. Like North American and European wolves, these African canines have a highly ordered social structure and hunt in packs. They are among the most efficient hunters, with a success rate topping 90 percent. Sadly, they are becoming rare in places in East Africa—where they were once common—mostly due to the fact that with huge home ranges, they often stray outside the protection of parks and reserves and are shot or poisoned by farmers and ranchers. They are more common in some of southern Africa's parks and reserves and in such places as Tanzania's Selous Game Reserve.

And then there is the birdlife. It is so varied and colorful that, if nothing else, you may become an ardent birder before your safari is done. From the ungainly marabou stork and the evil-eyed vultures to the elegant crowned crane and brilliantly colored malachite kingfisher, Africa's avian population is nothing short of spectacular. In this journal we've included checklists and some identifying photos of the more common species you are likely to find in East and southern Africa. There are so many that large volumes have been devoted to African birds, and we urge you to purchase some of these guidebooks to aid your identification of them.

Regardless of what you find, rare or common, your safari experience will be rich and rewarding. We hope you will use your safari journal to record your own adventures and observations to share with others. We also hope that you will help spread the word about the importance of preserving Africa's—and the world's—wild heritage. Hopefully, future generations will be able to experience the joy and wonders of being on safari—just as you have.

—The authors

A Maasai man carves a piece of wood. Living in parts of East Africa, the Maasai still dress in colorful traditional clothing and tend their cattle, goats, and sheep as they have for centuries. Some now adopt more-modern technology in the form of watches and even, yes, cell phones.

Places Not to Miss
in Africa

The African continent is rich and varied in its land features and corresponding bird and animal life. For the first-time safari traveler, there are several African countries that have the infrastructure and political stability to make your journey safe and enjoyable. What we present here is

intended only as a starting point for your own research. Nowadays the Internet can give a wealth of information on destinations and safari companies in each of the countries described here. However, before signing on with a tour company or safari outfitter, do some checking.

Check Out the Safari Company:

1. Ask how long the company has been in business.

2. Ask for references, particularly from those who reside in your own country and whom you can contact easily.

3. If it's a local or regional African company, find out if they have representation in your country—an office you can contact quickly to ask questions and make reservations.

4. Do some online research. Virtually all safari lodges, camps, and outfitters have Web sites to help you plan your safari.

5. Decide between fixed-departure tours (usually the less expensive option) and a custom designed itinerary (usually the more expensive option). Be aware that fixed-departure tours may be made up of large groups and include many people in each safari vehicle.

6. Do online research for special interest safaris: for birders, photographers, cultural tours, and so on. Many universities offer educational safaris with top-notch leaders. For serious photographers, the fewer people in the safari vehicle, the better (but also more expensive). And for photo tours, choose a tour leader with lots of safari experience.

7. Plan ahead! Many safari destinations have become so popular that they are booked many months in advance.

Botswana

Population: 1,640,115
Principal Languages: English (official), Setswana
Located: In southern Africa

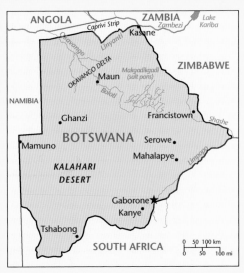

Neighbors: Nambia on the north and west, South Africa on the south, Zimbabwe on the northeast, Zambia on the north

Capital: Gaborone (199,000)

Currency: Pula

Of Interest: Botswana has some of Africa's greatest wildernesses and is noted for two major attractions: the Kalahari Desert and the Okavango Delta. The northern circuit is popular: Okavango, Moremi, Savuti, and Chobe National Park. Game viewing is excellent year-round. November to March is excellent for birders in the Okavango. High season is from July to October.

Flights: Can be arranged from Johannesburg, South Africa, directly to Maun in the north.

Web site: www.botswanaembassy.org

Kenya

Population: 33,829,590
Principal Languages: English, Swahili (both official), numerous indigenous

Located: In eastern Africa, on the coast of the Indian Ocean

Neighbors: Uganda on the west, Tanzania on the south, Somalia on the east, Ethiopia on the north, and Sudan on the northwest

Capital: Nairobi (2,575,000)

Currency: Shilling (KES)

Of Interest: The Rift Valley divides the highlands that run north to south through central Kenya. Highest point: Mount Kenya, at 17,058 ft. (5,199 m). Kenya is famous for its safaris and for its parks and reserves. Most

popular are Amboseli,
Masai Mara, Samburu,
Tsavo, and Lake Nakuru,
but there are other lesser
known places worth
visiting. Climate varies—the
Indian Ocean coast is very
humid, the interior uplands
cooler and drier. January to
March are the most
popular months for the
game reserves and parks. In
the upland interior, rains
normally fall from April to
June and October to

December. The great wildebeest migration arrives in the Masai Mara
from Tanzania in July and August.

Flights: International flights arrive daily
in Nairobi, and many game
reserves and parks can be
accessed by shorter flights from
the capital city.

Web site: www.kenyaembassy.com

Malawi
Population: 12,158,924
Principal Languages: Chicewa,

English (both
official), several
African languages
Located: In
southeast Africa
Neighbors: Zambia on the west,
Mozambique on the south and
east, Tanzania on the north
Capital: Lilongwe (587,000)
Currency: Kwacha (MWK)
Of Interest: Stretches 50 miles along
Lake Malawi. High plateaus and
mountains line the Rift Valley the

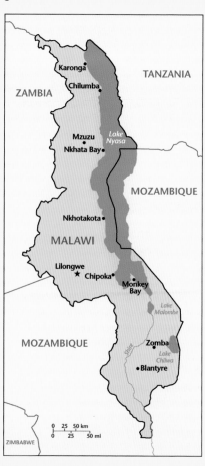

length of the country. Malawi is lesser known and has a less-well-developed tourism infrastructure. However, there are features worth visiting in any of the nine game reserves and in Lake Malawi National Park (noted for its birdlife). There is a dry season from April to November and a rainy season from December to March. The best game viewing occurs between April and November, with August the peak season for tourism.

Flights: International flights are into Lilongwe, the capital, from select European cities and from Johannesburg, South Africa.

Web site: www.malawi.gov.mw

Namibia

Population: 2,030,692

Principal Languages: English (official), Afrikaans, German, Oshivambo, Herero, Nama

Located: In south Africa on the coast of the Atlantic Ocean

Neighbors: Angola on the north, Botswana on the east, South Africa on the south

Capital: Windhoek (237,000)

Currency: Namibia Dollar (NAD)

Of Interest: The Kalahari Desert occupies the eastern part of the country. The Namib Desert is one of the driest on Earth, though it borders on the southern Atlantic Ocean. The coastal Namib Desert stretches up to 100 miles (160 km) inland. Part of the Namib are the

Sossusvlei Dunes, among the highest sand dunes in the world. Most popular is Etosha National Park, noted for its wildlife. Wildlife viewing is good throughout most of the year, but temperatures are most comfortable between April and November. The high season is from July until October.

Flights: Regularly scheduled commercial flights arrive daily in Windhoek, the capital, from Johannesburg, South Africa.

Web site: www.namibianembassyusa.org

Rwanda

Population: 8,440,820

Principal Languages: Kinyarwanda, French, English (all official), Swahili

Located: In east-central Africa

Neighbors: Uganda on the north, Congo (formerly Zaire) on the west, Burundi on the south, and Tanzania on the east

Capital: Kigali (656,000)

Currency: Franc (RWF)

Of Interest: Mountainous country, bordered by Lake Kivu on the west. Highest point: Mount Karisimbi, at 14,787 ft. (4,507 m). As of this writing, Rwanda has largely recovered from the tragic genocide in 1994. Tourists are once again returning to visit the famed mountain gorillas in Volcanoes National Park, one of only two places where it is feasible to visit them safely. (The other is Uganda.) Many safari travelers add a Rwandan gorilla visit as an extension to a safari in other countries, such as Tanzania and Kenya. April, May, June, and September through November are the rainiest months. The driest months are July and August, though in the rain forest habitat of the gorillas, rain is common anytime.

Flights: International flights arrive in the capital, Kigali, from select European cities and from Nairobi.

Web sites: www.rwandemb.org; www.rwanda1.com

South Africa

Population: 44,344,136

Principal Languages: Afrikaans, English, Ndebele, Pedi, Sotho, Swazi, Tsonga, Tswana, Venda, Xhosa, Zulu (all official)

Located: At the southern extreme of Africa

Neighbors: Namibia, Botswana, Zimbabwe on the north; Mozambique, Swaziland on the east; completely surrounds Lesotho

Capital: Cape Town (2,967,00)

Currency: Rand (ZAR)

Of Interest: South Africa is certainly one of the famous tourist destinations in

Africa, with numerous national parks and game reserves and well-known upscale private reserves and lodges. Most noted is Kruger, one of Africa's oldest and most visited national parks. While many species of birds and animals are distributed over wide ranges of the African continent, certain species are most common in South Africa and less common, or

not found at all, in East Africa. Wildlife viewing is good most of the year, but in the northern regions (Kruger and other reserves), May through September are the peak months.

The Great Escarpment rises beind the coastal plain and includes the Drakensberg Mountains. Much of the west is semidesert, while the east is mostly savannah grassland (veld).

Flights: International flights arrive in Johannesburg each day from many countries around the world.

Web sites: www.saembassy.org; www.gov.za

Tanzania

Population: 36,766,356

Principal Languages: Swahili, English (both official), Arabic, many local languages

Located: On the coast of East Africa

Neighbors: Kenya and Uganda on the north; Rwanda, Burundi, Congo (formerly Zaire) on the west; Zambia, Malawi, and Mozambique on the south

Capital: Dodoma (155,000)

Currency: Shilling (TZS)

Of Interest: The savannah plateau is divided by rift valleys and a north-south mountain chain. Highest point: Kilimanjaro, at 19,340 ft. (5,894 m), the highest point in Africa. In the past decade, Tanzania has emerged as one of Africa's top safari destinations. The most famous places are the Ngorongoro Conservation Area, Serengeti National Park, Tarangire National Park, and Mount Kilimanjaro. Tanzania also boasts Africa's largest game reserve, Selous, located in the southern part of the country.

A prime time to visit is from January to March, when the wildebeest migration is in the eastern Serengeti plains and the females are calving. A peak season is June and July, when the migration is in central Serengeti. April and May are the rainiest months. For Selous, June through August is a dry time to visit.

Flights: International flights arrive daily in Dar es Salaam, Tanzania's capital, from numerous cities world-wide. At northern Tanzania's Kilimanjaro Airport, closest to some of the parks, flights arrive daily from Amsterdam. It is also possible to arrive on many international flights in Nairobi, Kenya, and transfer to Arusha, in northern Tanzania.

Web sites: www.tanzaniaembassy-us.org; www.tanzania.go.tz

Uganda

Population: 27,269,482

Principal Languages: English (official), Swahili, Ganda, many Bantu and Nilotic languages, Arabic

Located: In east-central Africa

Neighbors: Sudan on the north; Congo (formerly Zaire) on the west; Rwanda and Tanzania on the south; and Kenya on the east

Capital: Kampala (1,246,000)

Currency: Shilling (UGS)

Of Interest: Most of the country is a plateau that ends in the west at the Great Rift Valley and the Ruwenzori Mountains. Lake Victoria covers southeastern Uganda. Uganda has

emerged from its sad and tragic history under Idi Amin's reign and is again rebuilding its once-famous tourism. This equatorial country has great variety, ranging from Queen Elizabeth National Park and the Ruwenzori Mountains in the west to Murchison Falls National Park, Uganda's largest national park, bisected by the Nile River. The most popular destination in recent years has been Bwindi Impenetrable Forest Reserve in the south, one of the few places left to visit mountain gorillas. The best times for visiting most of the parks are from late December to late February and from June to September.

Flights: International flights from select European countries arrive daily in Kampala.

Web sites: www.ugandaembassy.com; www.ugandaonline.net/government

Zambia

Population: 11,261,795

Principal Languages: English (official), Bemba, Tonga, Ngoni, and Lozi

Located: In south-central Africa

Neighbors: Congo (formerly Zaire) on the north; Tanzania, Malawi, and Mozambique on the east; Zimbabwe and Namibia on the south; Angloa on the west

Capital: Lusaka (1,394,000)

Currency: Kwacha (ZMK)

Of Interest: Both South Luangwa and North Luangwa National Parks are large, wild, and filled with game. Kafue National Park is not only Zambia's largest park,

it ranks among the largest reserves in the world and has retained a flavor of wild Africa. The seasons in Zambia range from cool and dry from May until August to hot and dry in September and October. November to April are the rainy months, and many of the parks close then because of limited access. Principal rivers are the Zambezi, Kafue, and the Luapula.

Flights: There are international flights into Lusaka from London's Gatwick and from Johannesburg, South Africa; Nairobi, Kenya; and Dar es Salaam, Tanzania.

Web sites: www.zambiatourism.com; www.travel.state.gov/travel/zambia.html

The preparations for a safari balloon trip can make for some great photo opportunities. You'll be up before dawn, and the filling of the balloons can be a challenge photographically, calling for high-speed film or a high ISO setting on your digital camera. It's a spectacular event.

Photography on Safari

hether you are a serious photographer or not, you will want to do the
best possible job of making a visual record of your journey—on film,
digitally, or with video. Here are some useful tips for photographing on safari.

General Information

Photo Equipment to Bring with You:

Patience

One of the things you learn with experience is that patience is a
great asset, especially when dealing with wildlife photography.
Slow down, wait, and watch. These are some of the last great
undisturbed ecosystems in the world. Hopefully you've chosen a
safari outfitter or tour company that doesn't rush from place to
place and gives you time to absorb it all.

Knowledge of the area

It's to your advantage to know as much as possible about the
places you'll be visiting, including behavior and habits of the
wildlife. Do some advance reading and look through magazines
and books to see what other photographers have done. We
suggest this not to have you imitate them, but rather to see
various approaches and techniques and to use this knowledge as
inspiration for your own creativity.

Knowledge of your camera equipment

The flight on the way to Africa is not a good time to begin
reading your camera instruction manual. You should have
thorough knowledge of your cameras and lenses long before you

leave home. Of course, bring your manual, because you may need to look up certain functions and features. But for the basics of shooting, practice, practice, practice—long before you leave home. Know your equipment.

If you buy a new lens or camera body before your safari, allow enough time to do some thorough testing. This is very important, not only to familiarize yourself with the equipment, but to reveal any flaws or problems (they do happen, even with new equipment).

The right equipment—lenses

If you are serious about your photography and have a camera with interchangeable lenses, you need to consider which lenses to bring. Most often, good wildlife shots are dependent on long telephoto lenses. Keep in mind that often the safari vehicles can get reasonably close to the animals because the animals have become tolerant of vehicles. However, in places where vehicles are not allowed to drive off-road, you may need a reasonably long telephoto lens for some shots. How long? For a fixed focal-length lens, 300mm is probably a minimum. With a fixed focal-length lens, you can use a 1.4X or 2X extender, making your 300mm a 420mm with a 1.4X extender and a 600mm with a 2X (not counting the "multiplier" effect on some digital cameras). If you choose a zoom lens, make it a 400mm at the longest focal length, for example, 80 to 400mm or 100 to 400mm zoom.

Should you buy a longer lens, a 500mm or 600mm? Longer telephoto lenses, especially with larger apertures, are very costly and very heavy and bulky. Only you can decide if it's worth the expenditure and also the hassle of getting a big lens into your carry-on bag. If you do a lot of wildlife and bird photography, it may be worth it.

For digital shooters, as you know, many camera bodies have a sensor smaller than 35mm dimensions and therefore have a "multiplier" effect of 1.4 or 1.5 or 1.6. So a 400mm lens effectively becomes a 560mm or a 600mm or a 640mm. This is more than adequate for a great many wildlife shots.

Mirror lenses? The advantages are that they are small, lightweight, and reasonably priced. Their disadvantages include a fixed aperture (usually f/8 for a 500mm focal length) and that out-of-focus bright highlights are rendered as doughnut-shaped rings.

Other lenses. There is a lot of opportunity to use lenses of other focal lengths. A good choice of lenses to bring, other than long telephotos, would be wide to medium zoom (21 to 35mm) and intermediate zoom (35 to 105mm or 80 to 200mm). If none of these zooms have macro focusing capability, you may want to bring a macro lens for insects, flowers, and so on.

Other equipment—tripods, beanbags, flash, etc.

Tripod and beanbag. Whether to bring along a tripod is a question that's difficult to answer. If you are used to using one and like to have it on hand, you should probably bring it—but keep it as small as possible. For most shooting in a vehicle, a beanbag provides good, steady support. You simply plop it on a window opening or the edge of a roof hatch and lay your camera and lens on it. You can buy a commercially made beanbag or make one yourself. For commercially made, go to www.kinesisgear.com and look up their SafariSack. Obviously, do not fill the beanbag before leaving home. Ask your safari outfitter to have some beans for you upon arrival. You may wish to contact your safari outfitter—some supply beanbags or other camera supports such as window clamps to aid photographers.

Flash. Aside from the built-in flash in most cameras, if you use larger flash units for fill-in lighting, by all means bring them (as long as they are not too big and bulky). There are many times you'll see birds sitting in trees, shaded by the canopy of leaves when a flash unit can fill in light very nicely. Kirk Enterprises (www.kirkphoto.com) makes a great Flash Xtender for use with 300mm and longer lenses. The unit weighs about three ounces and folds flat. There will also be times when you'll want to photograph interiors at lodges or at camp, and a flash unit is vital for that purpose.

Photo Vest. Vests are very useful, not just for field use but for wearing on flights as well. Why? Because the tough restrictions these days on weight and size of carry-ons can be a serious problem for photographers. A photo vest is like having a second carry-on, but one that won't be hassled over by airline people. You can stuff your vest with smaller lenses, bags of film, and so on. The vest is, after all, a piece of clothing that you are wearing. When you get on board, you can take it off and put in the overhead.

Backpack or camera bag. Many photographers favor a backpack with wheels and a handle for wheeling around airports. Many camera backpacks come with dividers inside to cushion lenses and camera bodies. If you have a lot of equipment to carry, you may find is necessary to strip out those dividers to make more space. For protection, wrap camera bodies and lenses in bubble wrap. The idea is to get as much vital equipment into your carry-on bag as possible. It's usually too risky to put cameras and lenses in your check-through luggage.

Plastic bags. It can be very dusty on safari. Bring a variety of plastic bags—one-gallon Ziplocs for film and certain lenses, jumbo or 2.5-gallon Ziploc bags for camera bodies, big garbage bags to cover camera bags and backpacks when the vehicle is traveling over roads. Bring enough of each to last the duration of the trip, because they get torn and beat up. Incidentally, it can also rain, so the plastic bags will help keep equipment dry as well.

Extra batteries, battery chargers, etc. Be sure to have enough extra camera batteries to get you through the trip. If you have familiarized yourself thoroughly with your equipment, you will have a good idea of how many rolls of film (or how many digital shots) you get on a set of batteries before replacing (or charging) them. This is especially important if you use non-rechargeable batteries. In all likelihood, you will not be able to find special batteries in any of the shops or lodges in Africa. You can usually find common ones, such as AA, but special lithium batteries are rare. Bring enough! If you use rechargeable batteries, bring at least two extra sets. This way you can have one set recharging at the camp or lodge while you are out on a game drive and have fully charged sets with you in the field.

Check with your safari outfitter about electricity in their camps and lodges. Undoubtedly, it will be 220 volts, so be sure your battery charger is dual voltage, i.e., 110/220 volts. The label on the charger will tell you. Most of them are dual voltage these days. If it is not dual voltage, you will need to bring a small transformer unit (available at Radio Shack and travel stores) to convert the 220 to 110 volts. In either case, you will also need adapter plugs. See page 5.

Also, for battery charging you may wish to bring one of the small cigarette lighter–style inverters. They are inexpensive and lightweight.

Information for Film Shooters

How Much Film?

Don't take a chance on running short—you may not be able to buy film in remote lodges and camps. Even if you are only a casual snapshooter, once on safari you're likely to find so many exciting subjects that you can easily run out of film before the trip's end. Double the amount you would ordinarily bring on a trip.

If you shoot print film, 100 or 200 speed is most useful. For dawn or dusk photographs (this is when certain wildlife are active), bring some additional rolls of 400 speed or higher.

If you shoot slide film, 100 speed is a good choice for most shooting. But also bring additional rolls or 200 and 400 for those darker lighting situations near dawn or dusk.

Keep in mind that slide film is not as forgiving of exposure errors as is print film. You need to be careful in using the camera's metering system. And for those very special shots, you may want to bracket exposures, that is, make one exposure at the meter's recommendation, then another that is 1/2 f-stop underexposed and a third shot that's 1/2 f-stop overexposed. If you do a lot of bracketing, double again the amount of film you bring. You never know what you're going to find or what kind of action may take place. Remember, it is far better to return with unused film than to run out while you are there.

The one thing to keep in mind when traveling by air with a lot of film is this: never, never, never put film in your check-through luggage. Keep it in your carry-on bag or your photo vest.

To reduce the volume and weight of the film in your carry-on, take the film cassettes out of the plastic film canisters. Put the cassettes in plastic Ziploc bags to pack in your carry-on bag. Put the plastic canisters in separate plastic bags and stash them in your check-through luggage. Later, on arrival, put the cassettes back in the canisters to protect them from dust and other damaging substances.

What about X-rays? In the United States, you can request a hand inspection and usually it will be honored (depending on how long the lines are and how hassled the inspectors). In most overseas airports, requests for hand inspection are denied. Is this something to worry about? Several years ago, Fuji and Kodak jointly initiated some testing using conventional airport X-ray units. Low- to medium-speed films (100 speed) were run through the units multiple times. Only when X-rayed up to 100 times did any damage appear.

What about lead bags? Forget it! First of all, if they block enough X-rays, the inspectors will make you take the film out of those bags and they'll run the film through the X-ray again. Second, a couple of those bags may weigh as much as the film, and you're adding more weight for no good reason.

The main concerns in caring for your film on safari are heat and dust. Keep the film in tightly closed plastic bags to avoid dust problems. Heat problems can be avoided by keeping film out of direct sunlight. It does get hot in the vehicles during the day, but the actual air temperature isn't bad enough to warrant refrigerating film. Just simple precautions are enough.

When changing film on a game drive, wait until the vehicle stops. Even driving across grasslands kicks up a certain amount of dust, and you should let the dust settle before changing film. It's also a good idea to have a small brush to whisk out the inside of the camera when you open it to change film. If you use compressed air, be very careful, because you could damage delicate shutter blades if you blast it directly on the shutter. At the end of each day, it's also a good idea to clean your camera body and lenses.

Information for Digital Shooters

Image Storage

When shooting digital, you have a couple of choices for storing image files: saving them as RAW or saving them as Jpegs. (On simpler cameras, you needn't worry about the choice, it will be Jpeg.) RAW files are large (8 to10 MB or more, depending upon the resolution of your camera). In addition, RAW files require post-processing on a computer to adjust white balance, contrast, and so on. Jpeg files are smaller, compressed files (1 MB, sometimes more or less, again depending upon the camera and degree of compression). Jpegs can be used as-is for printing and do not require post-processing. Regardless of whether you store images as RAW or Jpeg, the basic in-camera storage is a compact flash (CF) or secure digital (SD) card. These come in sizes of 256MB, 512MB, 1GB, 2GB, and even higher. Buy the higher capacity cards to reduce the number you have to carry.

RAW shooters: Because of the larger file sizes entailed here, you can't even think about storing all your pictures on CF or SD cards. These cards become merely intermediary storage devices. You will need something with much larger storage capacity—a laptop computer or a portable hard drive—to transfer the images from those cards. Even the smallest laptops can be a hassle to carry with you on a trip, though some people do. A smaller and lighter choice is a portable hard drive, such as the Epson P2000. This has a 40GB storage capacity and a big (almost four-inch) viewing screen of very high resolution for checking and evaluating images (and deleting them, when appropriate). Epson now has the P4000 with 80GB storage and the same screen. Even if you carried two of them, they would weigh less than the lightest laptop.

So, during the course of a day's shooting, as you fill up the CF or SD cards, transfer the images to the portable hard drive, erase the full cards, and continue shooting.

Jpeg shooters: Choose your camera's image quality setting to match your intended use for the pictures. If you want to make prints larger than 81/2 by 11 inches, set the camera for the highest image quality. For smaller final prints or for e-mailing images, use one of the intermediate quality settings. Consult your camera manual for information on how many images can be stored on various capacity cards. Then use this information to estimate how many storage cards you may need for the trip.

Example: For a 6 megapixel camera using the highest quality setting, you may be able to store up to 400 pictures on each 1 GB card. If you bring five 1GB CF or SD cards for storage, you can store a total of about 2,000 images. That's equivalent to about 55 rolls of 36-exposure film. Is that enough? Only you can decide that. With judicious editing, i.e., erasing the obviously bad shots, it may be enough.

Care of Equipment on Safari

Cameras, lenses, and digital storage devices must be protected against dirt and dust. Keep your CF or SD cards in the plastic cases they come with. And put these in closed Ziploc bags. Also, protect the cards against over-heating. Simply keeping them out of direct sunlight will help.

For those of you using digital single-lens reflex cameras (DSLRs) with interchangeable lenses, you must exercise care when changing lenses. Don't attempt to change lenses when the vehicle is moving (and possibly kicking up dust). The problem here is that you may end up with specks of dust on the image sensor, which will require careful cleaning.

Bring the proper equipment for cleaning your image sensor with you and follow carefully the instructions in your camera manual for carrying out such cleaning. Don't attempt any cleaning while out in the field. Wait to do that in camp or the lodge, where dust in the air is minimized.

If you bring a portable hard drive or a laptop for final image storage, keep either sealed in plastic bags against dust. Remember, both have hard drives with delicate moving parts, and they can be severely damaged by shock (for example, if they are dropped).

Technique and Subject Matter

Some Thoughts on Shooting Technique and Subject Matter on Your Safari:

Take your time. If the animals seem unconcerned by the presence of your vehicle, take advantage of this time to compose your pictures carefully. Wait for just the right pose or angle. Don't try to cram too many elements into your picture. Isolate a few elements for drama and impact.

Watch the lighting. Early morning and late afternoon are best for the quality of light. The direct overhead light at midday is very harsh and contrasty. Try to pick your best angle for lighting when you are approaching animals, then have your driver stop at the most favorable spot. Repeated starting of engines and movement of vehicles to jockey for a better position may cause even the most tolerant animals to leave. And always have the driver switch off the engine so that vehicle vibration won't interfere with picture-taking.

A polarizing filter is very effective for scenic shots, darkening and intensifying the color of the sky. The maximum effect is achieved when shooting at an angle of 90 degrees to the azimuth of the sun; the effect is minimal in other directions. Be sure to remove the polarizing filter when shooting wildlife, since it will have almost no effect on most subjects. More importantly, it will soak up the equivalent of about 11/2 f-stops of light, forcing you to use slower shutter speeds.

In most places on the African continent, you will observe some of the most spectacular sunrises and sunsets.

To Capture Sunrises and Sunsets:

1. Use a telephoto, or set your zoom lens to its longest focal length. This makes the sun larger in size for a more dramatic shot.

2. Take advantage of any landscape elements for dramatic silhouettes. A graceful acacia tree or any wildlife will enhance the composition of your picture.

3. Don't set your exposure for the sun itself. The resulting picture will probably be far too dark. Instead, aim the camera away from the sun and set the exposure for the sky, then lock the exposure setting and recompose the picture with the sun where you want it in the frame. You may also want to bracket exposures; that is, make shots slightly underexposed and slightly overexposed. This is often necessary to fine-tune exposure when shooting slide film.

Finally, we'd like to leave you with the cardinal rule of all good wildlife photographers: the welfare of the animal always comes first. Never approach too closely an animal stalking or hunting. When approaching any predators that are feeding, move as slowly and quietly as possible. If an animal is frightened away from its kill, another predator or scavenger may come along and steal it. When this happens, the very health of the animal and its young may be jeopardized. If any animal you approach behaves nervously and is about to flee, back off. Life in the forests and plains of Africa is stressful enough for wildlife without humans adding additional stress.

Safari njema. (Good journey in Swahili.)

ED SOKOLOSKY

Giraffes are always favorite animals for safari travelers. Though their unhurried grace makes them appear to be moving in slow motion, they can easily outrun most predators.

Journal Pages

Date _____

BOYD NORTON

EDWARD BORG

A vulturine guineafowl. This colorful bird is less common than the helmeted guineafowl and is found in dry thornbush in semidesert regions.

The bateleur is a bird of prey found in a wide variety of habitats, ranging from semi-desert to woodlands to savanna. They feed on small mammals, birds, frogs, and reptiles.

STEPHANIE SOKOLOSKY

A silverback mountain gorilla seems to be pondering a troubling question. These highly endangered great apes are found in Virunga National Park in eastern Democratic Republic of the Congo, Volcanoes National Park in Rwanda, and in Bwindi Impenetrable Forest Reserve in Uganda.

Date _____

STEPHANIE SOKOLOSKY

Zebras are gregarious animals. Often, great herds of them take part in the annual migration each year in East Africa. They are also very nervous and stampede at the slightest provocation—but then, wouldn't you, too, if there might be lions lurking in those bushes?

ED SOKOLOSKY

The stripe patterns of each zebra are unique—no two are alike. Biologists think the stripe patterns create visual confusion for predators when numerous zebras are running together.

Date _____

EDWARD BORG

The hippopotamus, or hippo, can weigh in at well over one ton. Hippos spend most of their time in water—in pools in rivers and lakes—leaving at night to graze on grasses. Territorial and aggressive, they fight among themselves frequently, with much bellowing. They are also dangerous to humans and are responsible for more human deaths in Africa than predators.

STEPHANIE SOKOLOSKY

The Nile crocodile is a dangerous customer indeed, lying in wait, submerged just beneath the surface of lakes and rivers. With great strength they grab an unwary wildebeest or gazelle or zebra, pulling the animal beneath the surface to drown it.

Date _____

The great white egret is always found near water, along shorelines of lakes, rivers, and marshes, where it feeds on frogs and fish.

The augur buzzard is a commonly seen bird of prey in East Africa, often perching on posts and dead trees in search of rodents.

It's one of the greatest wildlife spectacles left on Earth: the annual animal migration that takes place in the Serengeti ecosystem of Tanzania and Kenya. Each year, more than 1.5 million wildebeests, zebras, and other grazers make an 800-mile circuit in constant search of fresh grasses and water.

Date _____

The yellow-necked spurfowl is a member of the family of partridges that includes francolins and spurfowls. These chickenlike terrestrial birds are often heard early in the morning making a loud grating squawk, which serves as a warning against prowling predators.

Wildebeests are always on the move. As part of the great migratory herds, sometimes individuals seem playful. They will often run and jump and chase each other, apparently in an expression of fun.

Date _____

EDWARD BORG

Vervet monkeys are found over wide areas of sub-Saharan and southern Africa. Living in bands ranging in size from six to twenty, they eat mostly leaves and young shoots, flowers, fruits, roots, and seeds. Occasionally, they feed on insects, eggs, and nestlings. They are preyed upon by leopards, caracals, servals, and larger raptorial birds.

Date _____

EDWARD BORG

In many popular safari areas of Africa, hot-air ballooning is a popular activity. Launches are made at dawn, when there's only a slight breeze to carry balloons along safely. The sights can be spectacular, with views and perspectives not possible from the ground. Upon landing, a traditional champagne brunch is served out on the plains, sometimes within sight of wildlife.

ED SOKOLOSKY

A pride of lions looks longingly and hungrily at a distant group of grazers. Lions are gregarious members of the cat family, living in prides led by an elder female and consisting of numerous females and cubs. At about four years of age, males are kicked out of the pride to live alone and fend for themselves—although they often stay in the same region.

Date

Maasai teenage boys undergo a ritual of entering adulthood and becoming a *moran*, or warrior, by being circumcised.

A young Maasai girl wears beaded jewelry and earrings typical of her culture.

Some Maasai *bomas* allow visitors and charge a small fee, which provides income for members of the families here. In turn, visitors get to experience traditional Maasai songs and dances, including spectacular leaps into the air by young warriors.

Date _____

BOYD NORTON

A group of yellow-billed storks in the top of an acacia tree squabble over a perching place. Commonly found near lakes and marshes, these large birds are widespread throughout much of the African continent.

Date _____

ED SOKOLOSKY

Secretary birds often perch and build nests atop acacia trees. Their name is apparently derived from the resemblance of the bird's top feathers to the quill pens that eighteenth-century secretaries used to put in their hair buns. These birds of prey feed on snakes, lizards, and rodents.

ED SOKOLOSKY

Cape buffalo live in large herds, sometimes numbering fifty or more. With their formidable horns, they are among the more-dangerous animals in Africa. Though lions will some-times attack them, usually as a group, the cats are often injured—sometimes fatally—by these great beasts.

Date _____

Gerenuks live in dry thornbush country and feed on tender shoots and leaves of trees and bushes, which they reach by standing on their hind legs. They do not need water to drink, deriving all the moisture they need from their food.

An adult male lion in his prime, probably about seven to eight years of age. A dominant male may protect and service one or more prides of females, but his dominance will be usurped in a few years by a younger and stronger male.

The Serengeti Plain of East Africa is among the most famous of wildlife habitats. Vast and expansive, it seems to go on forever—and, in fact, the name is derived from a Maasai word, *serengit*, meaning "endless."

Date _____

ED SOKOLOSKY

A thirsty zebra at a waterhole. In parts of East Africa, zebras and wildebeest migrate hundreds of miles each year in search of water and fresh grasses, moving on as each region dries out.

EDWARD BORG

A topi atop a termite mound appears to be lecturing to a group of indifferent zebra. A common behavior for topi, it may be a combination of dominance assertion and looking out for predators. These sleek grazers are found over wide areas of East Africa. In southern Africa, a close relative is called the tsessebe, living in mopane forests and grasslands.

Date _____

The African fish eagle resembles the bald eagle of North America. Skilled at fishing, they swoop down from a nearby tree to catch an unwary fish in their talons.

A Kirk's dik-dik, a diminutive member of the antelope family. They are found in various regions of Africa, ranging from dry semiarid areas to dense bush country.

The Thomson's gazelle is the most common of the gazelles in East Africa. Living in herds of five to fifty or more, these groups consist of one male and a harem of females. The male must constantly fight off other males that would steal some of his females.

Date _____

BOYD NORTON

Two siblings, part of a family group, greet each other. Elephants often show affection toward each other by touching. During the 1980s, tens of thousands of elephants were killed by poachers for their ivory. The worldwide ban on ivory sales has brought poaching under control, and elephant populations are now increasing in many areas of Africa.

EDWARD BORG

Two male impalas fight over the leadership of a harem. Dominant males may have up to two dozen or more females in their group, and they must constantly defend against other males trying to take over or steal any of their females.

Date _____

The Nubian, or lappet-faced, vulture is the largest of African vultures. As scavengers, they are often found in the company of other vultures around carrion left by predators.

A snake eagle resting on the thorny branch of an acacia. These birds of prey feed on snakes, rodents, and small birds.

Three yellow-billed storks, a male and female with an immature youngster in the middle, seem to be striding with a purpose across grasslands adjacent to some marshes. These large storks are often found near lakes, streams, and marshlands, where they feed on small fish.

Date _____

A male kori bustard in courtship display. Puffing his neck feathers and holding his tail erect, he hopes to attract a female by displaying how handsome he is.

Olive baboons live in troops numbering from ten to a hundred or more. Grooming is a part of their social bonding, and hours each day are spent in this manner.

Dwarf mongooses often live in the tunnels of old termite mounds, where they rear their young. They feed primarily on insects but will also eat reptiles, small rodents, and young birds. Like other members of the mongoose family, the dwarf mongoose is gregarious and lives in colonies numbering fifteen or more.

Date _____

BOYD NORTON

A colorful African dawn finds a female elephant and youngster drinking from a small waterhole. The matriarch leader of an elephant family over time imparts her knowledge of where to find food and water to young members of the family.

Date _____

EDWARD BORG

Two male white rhinos in a semi-serious sparring match. Once widely distributed across the grasslands of tropical Africa, white rhinos are now confined to very limited areas in South Africa and parts of East Africa where, in well-protected reserves, they are once again increasing in number.

BOYD NORTON

Impalas, when panicked by the threat of a predator, can run very fast and make incredible leaps into the air in an apparent attempt to dodge a chasing leopard or cheetah. Jumps as high as ten feet and covering a distance of thirty feet or more are common.

Date _____

A yellow-billed hornbill. The actual color of the bill may range from yellow to deep orange. While incubating the eggs, the female is sealed (with mud) into a nesting hole in a hollow tree. The male feeds the female through a small hole.

A cinnamon-chested bee-eater. As the name implies, these colorful birds feed almost exclusively on bees, wasps, and hornets, which they swallow without regard for stings.

Black-backed jackals are common over many regions of East and southern Africa. Though thought of as scavengers because they are often found around predator kills, they are wily hunters and feed on hares, rodents, birds, insects, and eggs of both reptiles and birds.

Date _____

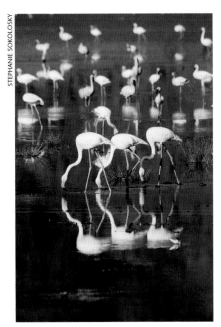

Lesser flamingos are always found around lakes of high alkaline and salt content, due to the algae and brine shrimp available there.

A gray heron uses the backs of sleeping hippos as a vantage point for spotting prey—small fish and frogs.

The saddle-billed stork is easily recognizable by its large size (standing more than five feet tall) and by its brilliantly colored beak.

Wild dogs or Cape hunting dogs can be thought of as Africa's wolves. Found over immense areas of east, central, and southern Africa, these canines live in packs.

Date _____

EDWARD BORG

Red-billed hornbills obtain their food almost exclusively on the ground, running about in search of beetles, grasshoppers, termites, and other insects, with an occasional lizard or bird's egg thrown in.

EDWARD BORG

The Grevy's zebra was once hunted for its hide, a beautiful pattern of fine stripes differing from those of the common or Burchell's zebra. This endangered species has a range limited to the drier regions of northern Kenya.

Date _____

A male ostrich tends a flock of newly hatched youngsters. The parent must stay near the young birds, for they are preyed upon by larger raptors and small predators, such as serval cats.

The crowned crane is one of Africa's most colorful birds and is, in fact, the national bird of Uganda. The male and female share the duty of feeding and rearing the young.

A mother giraffe nuzzles her youngster. Giraffe calves are vulnerable to predation by lions, leopards, and hyenas and are best protected by staying close to the mother and other adults in giraffe groups.

Date _____

Marabou storks are scavengers and often are found with vultures feeding on carrion left by predators. In many places, they've learned to hang around safari lodges and camps looking for leftover food.

The defassa waterbuck is found near water—lakeshores and marshes—and is distributed throughout central and East Africa. The related common waterbuck is found in parts of southern Africa.

In early morning light, this female leopard is surveying her domain. Solitary and elusive, these cats are widely distributed throughout sub-Saharan Africa and are at home in bush veld, forests, savannas, and arid country.

Date _____

A silverback mountain gorilla pauses during his morning feeding. These great apes, some weighing up to 400 pounds, are primarily vegetarians. Their diet consists of various plant leaves and vines. During the course of a day, a gorilla family roams slowly through their rain forest domain in search of favored plants.

The big yawn. This male lion is in his prime, about seven to eight years of age. This particular one is a resident of the Ngorongoro Crater in Tanzania, as indicated by the black color of his mane, a genetic trait of Ngorongoro lions.

Date _____

ED SOKOLOSKY

Bat-eared foxes are mostly nocturnal, though they are often found outside their dens in early morning. They feed mostly on insects, using their acute hearing (aided by those large ears) to locate the rustling of beetles and termites in the grasses.

STEPHANIE SOKOLOSKY

The honey badger (ratel) is one of the most fearless and strongest of small animals. Most large animals leave them alone because when cornered, the honey badger can spray a very strong-smelling liquid from its anal sacs. Its jaws lock onto its prey with a pitbull-like grip.

Date _____

BOYD NORTON

Agama lizards are distributed widely throughout much of Africa, though the variations in color are great. This pair (the male is on the right) is in Serengeti National Park in Tanzania. Even in East Africa, color variations are marked; some males have bright orange rather than red heads and upper body.

ED SOKOLOSKY

The Beisa oryx is found in the semiarid country of East Africa. The closely related gemsbok is distributed throughout a large area of South Africa and Namibia, again mostly in semiarid country and sometimes in mopane forests.

Date _____

The Grant's gazelle is found throughout East African savanna country. Sometimes in groups numbering dozens of animals, they are preyed upon by leopards, hyenas, and their young by cheetahs. In some areas, they have dark flank markings that might confuse them with Thomson's gazelles, but Grant's are larger and always have white over the rump.

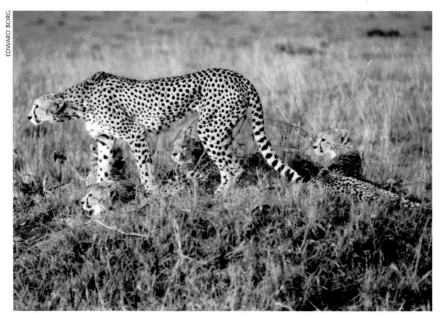

A female cheetah with three cubs has spotted some likely prey—possibly a Thomson's gazelle. When the cubs are small, they will remain hidden in the grass while the mother hunts. As they get older, cubs may follow along and, not as adept at stalking, sometimes spoil the hunt by alerting the potential prey.

Date _____

ED SOKOLOSKY

White rhinos are not necessarily white. The name is actually derived from the Dutch word *weidt*, meaning "wide." As opposed to the black rhino, which has a narrow mouth and prehensile upper lip, the white rhino's mouth is very wide. White rhinos are grazers, feeding on grasses. Black rhinos are browsers, feeding on twigs, leaves, and woody stems.

Date _____

ED SOKOLOSKY

The lilac-breasted roller is brilliantly colored, with iridescent feathers on its chin. They are often spotted on low tree and bush branches on the borders of woodlands with grasslands. From southern Tanzania to southern Africa, a related species, the racquet-tailed roller, is found in brachystegia and mopane woodlands.

BOYD NORTON

Mount Kilimanjaro, 19,340 feet in elevation, is Africa's highest mountain. Located in northern Tanzania near the Kenyan border, the surrounding plains are filled with wildlife.

Date _____

ED SOKOLOSKY

Elephants feed for up to sixteen hours a day, consuming hundreds of pounds of leaves, grasses, twigs, and even tree bark.

ED SOKOLOSKY

Cheetahs may hunt several times a day, depending upon the size of their last meal.

BOYD NORTON

A tawny eagle, light-colored phase. The tawny eagle's diet is largely fresh carrion of all kinds, but it will kill rodents, hares, and birds up to the size of guineafowl. It will also steal food from other raptors.

EDWARD BORG

Klipspringers are found throughout East and southern Africa, though only in rocky, hilly country and kopjes. Leatherlike pads on the bottoms of its hooves allow it the scramble and climb steep rocks.

Date

Young mountain gorillas often ride on their mothers' backs when the gorilla families are moving about the rain forest feeding on leaves and vines.

A young cheetah hides among the tall grasses while its mother goes off to hunt. About five to six weeks old, this youngster and its siblings will stay with their mother until they are fifteen to eighteen months old. The mortality rate of cheetah cubs is very high; they often fall prey to hyenas and lions.

Date _____

BOYD NORTON

EDWARD BORG

The bohor reedbuck is found in a band from East Africa across much of central Africa. The southern reedbuck is slightly smaller and lighter in color.

The blue monkey is primarily a forest dweller, found in certain select locations in East Africa, parts of Zambia, and in southeastern South Africa.

EDWARD BORG

Another spectacular African sunrise, this one in Tanzania's Serengeti National Park. The silhouetted umbrella acacia tree has become symbolic of the African continent.

Date _____

A house cat? The African wild cat is the size of the average domestic cat, but a wild (not feral) cousin, living over a great portion of Africa. In many parts of its range, it has different color variations, from light to dark, sometimes with faint spots.

The Coke's hartebeest is also called the kongoni. Like the topi and the red hartebeest, found in southern Africa, these large antelope are grazers found on the savanna and sometimes in lightly forested areas.

The lesser kudu (female shown here) is found on the savanna and in forested regions of East Africa. The closely related nyala is very similar in appearance, but its habitat is a restricted region in southeastern Africa. Both are members of the antelope family.

Date _____

EDWARD BORG

An option for adventurous safari travelers in northern Kenya is a camel trek led by Samburu people. Excursions may range from a few hours to an all-day trip.

BOYD NORTON

Among the smaller African cats is the serval. Found over large areas of sub-Saharan Africa, these elegant felines may weigh up to forty pounds. They prey on a variety of small animals, ranging from lizards to rodents to hares and birds as large as guineafowl.

Date _____

BOYD NORTON

BOYD NORTON

What appears to be cheetah laughter over a private joke is actually a yawn. The two cheetahs are subadults, probably close to a year old.

The baobab tree appears to be planted upside down. In the dry season, they drop their leaves. Some, like this giant in Botswana, may be 2,000 years old or older.

EDWARD BORG

In certain places in East Africa, lions have learned to climb trees in order to escape pesky insects and to stay cooler in breezes that might be blowing. This lioness is in Tanzania's Lake Manyara National Park.

Date _____

EDWARD BORG

Like little kids everywhere, this youngster seems determined to prevent its brother or sister from enjoying a midday nap. Young elephants up to several years of age may sleep lying down on the ground. Older adults rarely do this, sleeping while standing.

EDWARD BORG

Two male elephants engage in some semi-serious sparring. This game-playing may prepare them for a time when they need to defend themselves and assert dominance for mating rights over females.

Date _____

Greater kudu range widely over East and southern Africa. Their habitat is primarily forested areas and bush country. Only the males have horns.

Tsessebe appear to be a cross between topi and hartebeest; all are from the same family of antelopes. Found primarily in southern Africa, these sleek grazers rely on great speed to elude predators. This group is in the Moremi Game Reserve in Botswana.

Date _____

BOYD NORTON

ED SOKOLOSKY

The martial eagle is one of the larger raptors, with a wide distribution over much of East and southern Africa. In some areas, it is also called a snake eagle.

Two male impalas. Adult male impalas often congregate in "bachelor" herds sometimes numbering in the dozens. Each male awaits his chance to take over the harem of females from an older male.

ED SOKOLOSKY

Leopards blend into their surroundings well, especially when resting in trees. Often, unwary prey walk close to their perch, which allows the big cats to jump on and kill the animal from above.

Date _____

A lesser flamingo. The pink color of these large birds comes from their food—algae, rich in carotenoid pigments (like the pigments of carrots).

A Somali ostrich, found in northern Kenya, has a brilliant blue neck and legs compared to the brown or pink color of the common ostrich, found over the rest of the continent.

Black-winged stilts feed on small crustaceans, flies, and minnows along the edges of shallow lakes and marshes. They are often seen in association with flamingos.

Date _____

BOYD NORTON

Red lechwe are found only in certain regions of Zambia and northern Botswana. These members of the antelope family live in large groups, sometimes numbering in the hundreds. This small group is in a dryland area of the Okavango Delta.

BOYD NORTON

A defassa waterbuck has a wide, white circular rump patch as opposed to the common waterbuck, which does not have this marking. Though preyed upon by lions and leopards, these cats may mostly avoid waterbucks because the meat has an unpleasant taste due to oily, musky secretions in the skin.

Date _____

ED SOKOLOSKY

The hammerkop is widely distributed throughout Africa wherever there is water nearby. Remarkably for such a relatively small bird, they build immense nests of sticks in the forks of large trees, usually near water.

STEPHANIE SOKOLOSKY

Warthogs may not win any beauty prize, but they are favorites of safari travelers—perhaps because of their ungainliness. Running with their long antennalike tails in the air, they scamper through the grasslands, speedy enough to outrun many predators. Though small prey for lions, the big cats seem to consider them a delicacy.

Date _____

BOYD NORTON

Among the many weavers found across Africa, the Speke's weaver is common in East Africa, building—or rather weaving, out of grass—its pendulous nest in acacia trees.

BOYD NORTON

Red-and-yellow barbet. Barbets are related to woodpeckers, though they primarily eat fruit. This colorful bird is found throughout East Africa, preferring arid and semiarid country. It is commonly seen at the visitor center on the rim of Olduvai (Oldupai) Gorge in Tanzania.

Date _____

ED SOKOLOSKY

BOYD NORTON

This large nocturnal bird, the Verreaux's eagle owl, is sometimes spotted in the daytime, deep under the branches of an acacia tree.

Ouch! Black rhinos feed on leaves and stems of many plants, including this young and thorny acacia. Apparently their leathery tongues and lips are impervious to the thorns.

BOYD NORTON

Ground hornbills, found over much of East and southern Africa, spend much of their time walking, foraging for lizards and snakes, their favorite food. They also eat fallen fruit from trees.

Date _____

BOYD NORTON

Gliding quietly along the waterways of the Okavango Delta in a native mkoro gives visitors an opportunity to observe close-up many of the plants, animals, and aquatic species of this fascinating region.

BOYD NORTON

Throughout lightly wooded areas of central and southern Africa, roan antelope live in harem groups numbering up to fifteen or so and led by a dominant male. This one was photographed in Moremi Game Reserve in northern Botswana.

Date _____

A hippo takes offense at some transgression by a neighbor. These huge mammals often fight among themselves, often over dominance or invasion of personal space.

The largest of Africa's waterfowl, the spur-winged goose, is also one of the most colorful. Widespread throughout the continent, it is always found near water—swamps, lakes, and rivers.

Three-month-old spotted hyena cubs outside their den. At five months of age, the cubs begin to eat meat from kills made not far from the den. Both scavenger and skilled hunter, adult hyenas have jaws powerful enough to crush the bones of large animals.

Birds of Africa

Superb Starling

Fischer's Lovebird

Lilac-breasted Roller

Speke's Weaver

Glossy Ibis

Secretary Bird

Goliath Heron

Sacred Ibis

European Roller

PHOTOS BY EDWARD BORG, BOYD NORTON, ED SOKOLOSKY, AND STEPHANIE SOKOLOSKY

In Africa, south of the Sahara, there are more than 1,700 varieties of birds. Below are some of the most common. A bird book will be of great assistance.

Bird Checklist

Species	Date	Location
Avocet, Black-capped		
Babbler		
Arrow-marked		
Brown		
Barbet		
Black-collared		
Crested		
D'Arnaud's		
Double-toothed		
Green		
Red-and-yellow		
Bateleur		
Batis, Chin-spot		
Bee-eater		
Carmine		
Cinnamon-chested		
European		
Little		
Swallow-tailed		
White-fronted		
White-throated		
Bishop		
Black-winged		
Red		
Bittern		
Boubou		
Crimson		
Slate-colored		
Tropical		
Brubru		
Bulbul		
Black-eyed		
Cape		
Garden		
Red-eyed		

Bird Checklist

Species	Date	Location
Bulbul, *continued*		
Yellow-vented		
Bunting, Golden-breasted		
Bush-shrike		
Gray-headed		
Rosy-patched		
Bustard		
Black-bellied		
Denham's		
Jackson's		
Kori		
Stanley's		
Buzzard		
Augur		
Jackal		
Lizard		
Canary		
African Citril		
Streaky		
Yellow-fronted		
Chat		
Mocking Cliff		
Robin		
Stone		
Cisticola		
Hunter's		
Rattling		
Coot, Red-knobbed		
Cordon-bleu, Red-cheeked		
Cormorant		
Cape		
Great		
Long-tailed		
Reed		
White-breasted		
Coucal		
Black		
White-browed		

Birds of Africa

Little Bee-eater

Abdim's Stork

Dark Chanting Goshawk

African Spoonbill

Black-bellied Bustard

Blacksmith Plover

Hooded Vulture

Carmine Bee-eater

Crowned Plover

PHOTOS BY EDWARD BORG, BOYD NORTON, ED SOKOLOSKY, AND STEPHANIE SOKOLOSKY

Bird Checklist

Species	Date	Location
Courser		
Temminck's		
Two-banded		
Crake		
African		
Black		
Crane		
Black Crowned		
Blue		
Crowned		
Wattled		
Crombec, Red-faced		
Crow		
House		
Pied		
Cuckoo		
African Emerald		
Diederik		
Jacobin		
Red-chested		
Cuckoo-shrike, Black		
Darter, African		
Dove		
Emerald-spotted		
Laughing		
Mourning		
Namaqua		
Red-eyed		
Ring-necked		
Drongo, Fork-tailed		
Duck		
Knob-billed		
Red-billed		
White-faced		
Yellow-billed		
Eagle		
African Fish		
African Hawk		

Bird Checklist

Species	Date	Location
Eagle, *continued*		
Black-breasted Snake		
Booted		
Brown Snake		
Crowned		
Long-crested		
Martial		
Steppe		
Tawny		
Egret		
Black		
Cattle		
Great White		
Little		
Yellow-billed		
Falcon		
African Pygmy		
Lanner		
Peregrine		
Firefinch, Red-billed		
Flamingo		
Greater		
Lesser		
Flycatcher		
Blue		
Paradise		
Spotted		
White-eyed Slaty		
Francolin		
Coqui		
Crested		
Red-billed		
Gallinule, Purple		
Gannet, Cape		
Go-away Bird		
Bare-faced		
White-bellied		

Bird Checklist

Species	Date	Location
Goose		
African Pygmy		
Egyptian		
Spur-winged		
Goshawk		
Dark Chanting		
Pale Chanting		
Grebe		
Black-necked		
Little		
Greenshank		
Grenadier, Purple		
Guineafowl		
Crested		
Helmeted		
Vulturine		
Gull		
Gray-headed		
Hartlaub's		
Sooty		
Hammerkop		
Harrier		
African		
Montagu's		
Helmet-shrike		
White		
White-rumped		
Heron		
Black		
Black-headed		
Goliath		
Green-backed		
Night		
Purple		
Squacco		
Honeyguide		
Greater		
Lesser		

Bird Checklist

Species	Date	Location
Hoopoe		
Hornbill		
Abyssinian Ground		
African Gray		
Black-and-white Casqued		
Crowned		
Ground		
Red-billed		
Silvery-cheeked		
Southern Yellow-billed		
Trumpeter		
Von der Decken's		
Ibis		
Glossy		
Hadada		
Sacred		
Jacana, African		
Kestrel		
Gray		
Lesser		
Rock		
Kingfisher		
Brown-hooded		
Giant		
Gray-hooded		
Malachite		
Pied		
Striped		
Woodland		
Kite		
Black		
Black-shouldered		
Korhaan		
Black-bellied		
Red-crested		
Lammergeier (Mountain Vulture)		
Lark		
Fischer's Sparrow		

Bird Checklist

Species	Date	Location
Lark, *continued*		
Red-capped		
Red-winged Bush		
Rufous-naped		
Longclaw		
Rosy-breasted		
Yellow-throated		
Lourie, Gray		
Lovebird		
Fischer's		
Lilian's		
Mannikin, Bronze		
Martin, Rock		
Moorhen, Common		
Mousebird		
Blue-naped		
Red-faced		
Speckled		
Nightjar		
Fiery-necked		
Gabon		
Oriole		
Black-headed		
Golden		
Osprey		
Ostrich		
Masai		
Somali		
Owl		
African Scops		
Spotted Eagle		
Verreaux's Eagle		
White-faced Scops		
Owlet, Pearl-spotted		
Oxpecker		
Red-billed		
Yellow-billed		

Bird Checklist

Species	Date	Location
Parrot		
African Gray		
Brown		
Cape		
Gray		
Pelican		
Great White		
Pink-backed		
Piapiac		
Pigeon, Speckled		
Pipit		
Golden		
Richard's		
Plantain-eater, Gray		
Plover		
Blacksmith		
Crowned		
Gray		
Kittlitz's		
Spur-winged		
Three-banded		
Wattled		
Quail		
Common		
Harlequin		
Quelea		
Cardinal		
Red-billed		
Raven, White-necked		
Roller		
Abyssinian		
European		
Lilac-breasted		
Purple		
Rufous-crowned		
Rook, Cape		
Ruff		
Sanderling		

Bird Checklist

Species	Date	Location
Sandgrouse		
Black-faced		
Burchell's		
Chesnut-bellied		
Namaqua		
Yellow-throated		
Sandpiper, Common		
Secretary Bird		
Seedeater, Streaky		
Shoebill		
Shrike		
Fiscal		
Gray-backed Fiscal		
Long-tailed Fiscal		
Magpie		
White-crowned		
Yellow-billed		
Silverbird		
Skimmer, African		
Sparrow		
Cape		
Gray-headed		
Rufous		
Spoonbill, African		
Spurfowl		
Gray-breasted		
Red-necked		
Yellow-necked		
Starling		
Ashy		
Golden-breasted		
Greater Blue-eared		
Hildebrandt's		
Purple		
Red-winged		
Rüppell's Long-tailed		
Superb		
Wattled		

Bird Checklist

Species	Date	Location
Starling, *continued*		
Western Long-tailed		
Stilt, Black-winged		
Stint, Little		
Stonechat, Common		
Stork		
Abdim's		
African Open-billed		
Marabou		
Saddle-billed		
White		
Woolly-necked		
Yellow-billed		
Sugarbird, Cape		
Sunbird		
Amethyst		
Beautiful		
Black		
Bronze		
Collared		
Double-collared		
Hunter's		
Malachite		
Mariqua		
Orange-breasted		
Scarlet-chested		
Tacazze		
Variable		
White-bellied		
Swallow		
European		
Lesser Striped		
Red-rumped		
Wire-tailed		
Swamphen, Purple		
Swift		
African Palm		
European		

Animal Checklist

Species	Date	Location
Aardvark		
Aardwolf		
Antelope		
Roan		
Sable		
Baboon		
Anubis (Olive)		
Chacma		
Savannah		
Yellow		
Badger, Honey (Ratel)		
Bat		
Epauletted Fruit		
Flying Fox		
Hammer-headed		
Straw-colored Fruit		
Blesbok		
Bongo		
Bontebok		
Buffalo		
African		
Cape		
Bushbaby (Galagos)		
Greater		
Lesser		
Bushbuck		
Bushpig		
Caracal (African Linx)		
Cat		
African Golden		
African Wild		
Small-spotted		
Cheetah		
Chimpanzee		
Civet, African		
Crocodile		
Dik-dik		
Guenther's		
Kirk's (Damara)		

Animal Checklist

Species	Date	Location
Dog		
African Wild		
Cape Hunting		
Duiker		
Abbott's		
Aders'		
Black-fronted		
Blue		
Bush		
Harvey's		
Peters'		
Red (Natal)		
Yellow-backed		
Eland		
Elephant		
Elephant Shrew		
Golden-rumped		
Rufous		
Fox		
Bat-eared		
Cape		
Gazelle		
Bright's		
Grant's		
Peters'		
Thomson's		
Gemsbok (Oryx)		
Genet		
Bush		
Large-spotted		
Small-spotted		
Gerenuk (Walker's Gazelle)		
Giraffe		
Masai		
Reticulated		
Rothschild's		
Gorilla		
Grysbok		
Cape		

Animal Checklist

Species	Date	Location
Grysbok, *continued*		
Sharpe's		
Hare		
Cape		
Scrub		
Hartebeest		
Coke's (Kongoni)		
Jackson's		
Lelwel		
Lichtenstein's		
Red		
Hedgehog, African		
Hippopotamus		
Hog, Giant Forest		
Hyena		
Brown		
Spotted		
Striped		
Hyrax (Dassies)		
Bush		
Rock		
Tree		
Impala (Pala)		
Jackel		
Black-backed		
Golden		
Side-striped		
Klipspringer		
Kob		
Kudu		
Greater		
Lesser		
Lechwe		
Black		
Red		
Leopard		
Lion		
Mangabey		

Animal Checklist

Species	Date	Location
Mongoose		
Banded		
Black-tipped		
Dwarf		
Marsh		
Slender		
White-tailed		
Monkey		
Black Mangabey		
Black-and-white Colobus		
Blue		
De Brazza's		
Patas		
Red Colobus		
Red-tailed		
Samango		
Sykes'		
Tana Mangabey		
Vervet		
Nyala		
Okapi		
Oribi		
Oryx		
Beisa		
Fringe-eared (Gemsbok)		
White		
Otter		
Clawless		
Spotted-necked		
Pangolin		
Ground		
Tree		
Porcupine		
Potto		
Puku		
Ratel (Honey Badger)		
Reedbuck		
Bohor		
Mountain		

Animal Checklist

Species	Date	Location
Reedbuck, *continued*		
Southern		
Rhebok, Gray		
Rhinocerous		
Black		
White		
Sable, Roosevelt's		
Serval		
Shrew, Otter		
Sitatunga		
Springbok		
Springhare		
Squirrel		
Ground		
Striped Ground		
Southern African Tree		
Steenbok		
Suni		
Topi (Karrigan)		
Tsessebe		
Warthog		
Waterbuck		
Common		
Defassa		
Weasel, African Striped		
Wildebeest		
Black		
Blue (Brindled Gnu)		
White-bearded (White-bearded Gnu)		
Zebra		
Burchell's		
Cape Mountain		
Grant's		
Grevy's		
Plains		
Zorilla		

Words and Phrases

Swahili
Spoken in many East African countries

Greetings/General Usage:

Hello . . . .*Jambo*

Good-bye (to more than one) . . . .*Kwa heri (kwa herini)*

Thank you (very much) . . . .*Asante (sana)*

Yes . . . .*Ndiyo*

No . . . .*Hapana*

Please . . . .*Tafadali*

Good morning . . . .*Habari ya asubuhi*

Good night . . . .*Lala salama*

How are you? . . . .*U hali gani?*

I am good or fine (very). . . . .*Mzuri or Mjema (sana)*

Welcome . . . .*Karibu*

May I come in? . . . .*Hodi?*

You may come in. . . . .*Karibu*

No problem . . . .*Hakuna matata*

(counting) *1–Moja, 2–mbili, 3–tatu, 4–nne,*
5–tano, 6–sita, 7–saba, 8–nane,
9–tisa, 10–kumi

Where, when, what, who, why . . . .*Wapi, lini, nini, nani, kwa nini*

How much is that? . . . .*Ni ngapi?*

What time is it? . . . .*Saa ngapi?*

Wildlife:

Bird . . . .*Ndege*

Buffalo . . . .*Nyati*

Cheetah . . . .*Duma*

Crocodile . . . . *Mamba*

Elephant . . . . *Tembo or Ndovu*

Giraffe . . . . *Twiga*

Hippo . . . . *Kiboko*

Hyena . . . . *Fisi*

Leopard . . . . *Chui*

Lion . . . . *Simba*

Rhino . . . . *Kifaru*

Snake . . . . *Nyoka*

Warthog . . . . *Ngiri*

Wildebeest . . . . *Nyumbu*

Zebra . . . . *Punda milia*

Kinyarwanda
Common language of Rwanda

Greetings/General Usage:

Hello . . . . *Muruho*

Good-bye (to more than one) . . . . *Murabeho*

Thank you (very much) . . . . *Murakoze (cyahe)*

Yes . . . . *Yego*

No . . . . *Oya*

Please . . . . *Mbabarira*

Good morning . . . . *Mwaramutse (ho)*

Good night . . . . *Muramuke (ho)*

How are you? . . . . *Amakuru (ki)?*

May I come in? . . . . *Hodi?*

You may come in. . . . . *Murisanya*

No problem . . . . *Nta Kibazo*

Wildlife:

Gorilla(s) . . . . *Ingagi*

Forest . . . . *Ishyamba*

Bamboo . . . . *Umugano*

Rangers, trackers . . . . *Abagaradi*

Guide . . . . *Umugide*

African Wildlife

Malachite Kingfisher

Common Duiker

Hoopoe

Silvery-cheeked Hornbill

Rock Hyrax

Baby Elephant

Tawny Eagle

White Pelican

PHOTOS BY EDWARD BORG, BOYD NORTON, ED SOKOLOSKY, AND STEPHANIE SOKOLOSKY

African Adventures — in books!

When Elephants Fly
One Woman's Journey
from Wall Street to Zululand
Carol Batrus

A memoir that speaks to all who have felt burnt out, stuck in a rut, or unchallenged by the aspect of daily life—regardless of their personal success.
1-55591-565-5
6 x 9, 256 pages, b/w photos, PB $15.95

Tales of the Full Moon
Sue Hart • Illustrated by Chris Harvey

Short stories of African animals. Each story is told by Spinosa, a spider, who weaves together the antics of the animals that live in the African bush around her.
1-55591-582-5
7.5 x 10.5, 96 pages, full color, PB $16.95

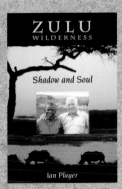

Zulu Wilderness
Shadow and Soul
Ian Player

An adventure of both the mind and spirit, this book is an engaging personal memoir of Ian Player's life work as a conservationist, his partnership with Magqubu Ntombela, and their successful effort to save the white rhino.
1-55591-363-6 • 6 x 9, 320 pages, PB $21.95

South African Passage
Diaries of the
Wilderness Leadership School
Preface by Laurens van der Post
Introduction by Ian Player

South African teenagers write of personal transition through wilderness experiences.
1-55591-009-2
5 x 7, 208 pages, 12 b/w illustrations, HB $13.95

FULCRUM PUBLISHING
WWW.FULCRUMBOOKS.COM
800-992-2908 • 303-277-1623
GOLDEN, COLORADO, USA